Cabin Woolgathering

By Beth Dunkin

Copyright © 2004 by Elisabeth Dunkin

ISBN 0-7414-1957-2

Published by:

INFINITY
PUBLISHING.COM

1094 New Dehaven Street
Suite 100
West Conshohocken, PA 19428-2713
Info@buybooksontheweb.com
www.buybooksontheweb.com
Toll-free (877) BUY BOOK
Local Phone (610) 941-9999
Fax (610) 941-9959

Printed in the United States of America

Printed on Recycled Paper

Published May 2004

Cabin Woolgathering

The author has traveled from her childhood home in Oklahoma City and then her adult home in Tulsa, Oklahoma to a romantic spot on a chain of lakes in west central Minnesota. She is part of a third generation to enjoy an "old cabin" located in Alexandria, Minnesota on Lake Le Homme Dieu. One of her greatest pleasures is watching her four beautiful adult daughters, their husbands and children playing at the lake. She is a student of the Bible and has spent decades both teaching and learning this ancient text.

Illustrations by Nadine Peters,
one of God's creative angels.

Cabin Woolgathering

Woolgathering is defined as absent-minded indulgence in fanciful daydreams.

Summer begins with the slam of a screen door, the frantic run of the black Lab and the unique smell of the hibernating cabin. In May there is new birth everywhere with  tiny hummingbirds, scampering, little bunnies and quicker-than-the-eye baby chipmunks, chipmunks which the black Lab thinks are his personal toys to chase. Then, of course, there is the lilac. For one week around the end of May, the cabin is filled with the dreamy smell of lilacs pruned from a stranger's bush. The gardens are just beginning and look so pathetic, but then, I forget that they are just welcoming growth as I am. Does one grow when one only goes to the grocery store seven times all summer, or somehow survives life without driving a car for ten days, or goes for forty-eight hours without hearing a human voice? I think so. This is my place for renewal, for filling up, for life in abundance. 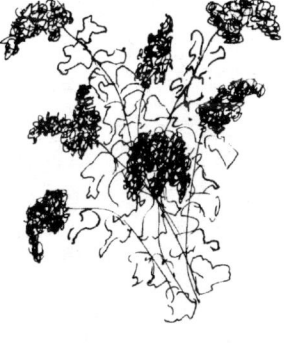 This is my little corner of God's world. My spot to hug the

sounds and smells, the colors and shapes, the feelings and emotions which act as a retreat from the clutter of man's world and embraces God's paradise as I know it.

There is much to do to show my appreciation that one more summer has been placed in my lap: gutters to clean, leaves to get off the ferns, lawns to care for, trees to prune, and of course, the never-ending slap of paint to freshen up and fill the cracks of the old cottage. Does one call her a cottage or a cabin? I guess it does not matter as long as she is what she is. The smaller places in the back are called bungalows,  usually built on the location or foundations of the old ice houses or outhouses. Most all of the older cabins never had foundations of cement but rather originally were placed on stilts. They have crawl throughs which we now pay handsomely for plumbers to crawl under. Much of the work of opening up the cabin has already begun long before I arrive. Bird feeders have been placed and filled for the little Yellow Finch players to arrive and begin their summer show. Electricity has been turned on. Water pipes (which were drained for the brutal winters) have now been opened and filled with water from the wells. Gas water heaters have gone on to make cleaning

.

water hot, and the furniture and windows are unveiled. After a thorough cleaning of dust bunnies and a washing of all linens, the tarps, boards, coverings of all kinds are removed from the windows. When windows are washed, hammered open and then propped open with a stick, the cabin is ready to open up her old wrinkled arms to welcome her guests.

With each storm of summer, I wonder in amazement how the "old girl" can withstand the howling winds and the torrential rains. As I duck with each clap of thunder, I comfort myself by remembering that "she does." She does survive and has for a hundred years. The nurturing soul of the old cabin is eternal, not made of boards and old rusty nails. She shouts her power by surrendering to the blowing rains, bowing to the winds that come over the lake like an awesome black wall approaching, making it necessary to place pans and buckets under her open wounds. There is that panic of "Oh my gosh! What do we do?"

 which is overcome by sitting down, accepting what we cannot change, surrendering as she does and listening to the drip.

There is always the day after the storm when we timidly venture from our little cabins to survey the damage done to the diving tower, docks and boats. This is the day of hundreds of

sticks all over the yards. Like the children's game of 'pick up sticks,' away we go dragging the little red wagon behind us collecting the sticks, sticks which long ago were put into the wood stove or fireplaces. This year the children have made a fire pit so I have a place to put the pruned material rather than sneaking to the back woods to unload the dead on someone else's land. But then, no one owns the land. Thinking that the land is owned by ourselves is a lie our civilization tells us. We are only stewards of the land, and stewards for only a short time. When the old cabins were part of a fishing lodge in the early 1900's, they were rented and each had a name like "Kilcare," "Take-home-a-tan," "BlueBird," "U-need-a-rest." They didn't have names of ownership, just names of character. The question is how can I keep the character of the old place from falling down without changing her? I guess my part is to keep the shell that houses her soul without scaring her soul off. An 'old soul' is a good way to think of the cabin. For so many years the thinking has been "if it is old or broken, take it to the cabin." She doesn't seem to have many new things which I guess is one reason I buy for her. Little things. Mostly knick knacks which make me laugh for a year or so, then seem like clutter.

I often think I would like to blacktop the driveway. Simply I guess to make it look neater but then rumor has it that doing so will raise taxes. Taxes are one

thing we all complain about, but we love the appreciation of the land. The monetary value is not in the buildings but in the land. We fear the selling of property because we fear new owners will tear down the charming old and build the new. The integrity of the land and shoreline has become a top priority. Because of the dramatic increase in value, the population on the land has also risen. There are times I am beginning to feel as if I am in a suburb. That is on the weekend, but during the week the embracing quiet returns.

Each year we lose trees but plant new ones new ones for the next generation to build tree forts to hide them from the adult world. That new generation of laughing children, playful, barking dogs, and the roaring speedboats that are never fast  enough, big enough or new enough will be here before we know it. The older I get the more I seem to dislike what I call the 'rape of God's lake' by those toys we use for our instant gratification, blasting through the innocent serenity of the loons, leaving gasoline trails in their wake. It is not just the new generation; I did it too. Must be a people thing pretending to be God going so fast, owning it all.

There is a maturity level where one leaves the thinking "to tear it all down and build new" and moves into the desire "to fix up the old." Maybe it is not so much age or maturity but rather  that time when precious memories begin to outnumber future visions. My grandchildren are now a fifth generation. They have no idea of the many spirits that have gone before them, but they add their own as they splash in wading pools graduating to the lake, trying to capture the wild whether it is fireflies or chipmunks. While they tell their stories around the campfires and eat their smores and play their games, games of Kick the Can, Snipe Hunting, Hide and Go Seek, Duck-Duck-Goose, poker, cards and the perpetual puzzles, they add their own spirit. Each spirit seems to stand on the shoulders of the ones before creating pyramids of gaiety.

There are neighbors where one remembers the grandparents of one's friend, lifelong friends literally from cradle on who see each other every summer, when one doesn't appear to have a care in the world. But then that is just an illusion. At the lake there is no generation gap and we are like little children in the park playing as if we never had to go home to do homework. Could it be that our playing is our homework? Nothing fills my heart more than watching my children play. Of course they have limits and I want them to be safe, but I do not care how they play or what they play with as long as it is joyful, safe and to their hearts' content. I wonder if God is like that . . . loving our play? Does playing bring back our innocence? We all feel so safe at the cabin. Are we that far removed from the scary world or is innocence bliss? Whatever the reason, we all feel it. There is an openness and freedom which comes with the cabin. There are no fences to the east or west, no security systems for the houses, just the lake to the south and the back road to the north lined with the foreboding woods. Natural, safe boundaries undetected by the innocent eye of a child seem to make us all feel safe.

The woods are really not that foreboding and certainly not that thick, although they do house deer who brave the road every now and then to eat the carefully planted hostas in the gardens. The woods are remote enough for the majestic eagles to build their nests high in the trees. Eagles are close enough to entertain us with their fishing and soaring over our lake or rather their lake. The woods used to come up to the back doors of the cabins and the road went between the lake and the cabins but that was a long time ago. Long ago before government red tape would prevent the cabin men from deciding one day to move the road "way back in the woods." It was not just a spur of the moment decision. In the early nineteen hundreds, the cabin men had held their breath more than once as overly excited children darted from their mothers' reach to the calling waters of the lake just as one of the old cars (looking as if it were out of control) came bouncing down the dirt road.

Slowly the woods going to the new road became back  yards at least to the road, but on the other side of the road the woods remained. There is a secret lake in the woods and a path that leads to Grandmother LeComptes' fern supply. It is to this lake

8

in the woods the young girls would go to wash and dry their young maidens' secrets. The story is told of the ornery boys going "rag" hunting in these secret woods much to the horror of the girls. Some things never change.

So little has changed, yet so much has changed. Hot and cold faucets have replaced the old pumps at the back doors, pumps that had to be primed as we patiently waited for the cold, cold well water to rise. Now those pumps act as door stops or garden art. The old boat docks with the heavy rollers on the end have been replaced with elec-  tric lifts. The ice houses on the lake have gone and now we have refrigerators. The boat houses have been replaced by professional storage units. Screened-in porches have been glassed in, and decks have been built and then screened in. In that time long ago, individual bedrooms as we know them were scarce; for everyone's bed was placed on the cool lakeside screened porch which had a floor that sloped toward the screens to let the rain water out. Wood stoves were replaced by electric or gas stoves, nature's choice of air was replaced by heaters and air conditioners, and of course outhouses were replaced by flushable toilets. The old kerosene lamps, which my mother had to clean every morning, were replaced by the electric lights. I still have the old lamps

ready to light just in case of an exciting electrical outage. Huge bright colored water rafts replaced the old black Army Surplus Navy boat, which as children we would jump off of for hours on end, turning our swimsuits tire black. Some change is good as long as we remember the way it was and why.

Does the old teach the new or do the new teach the old? Perhaps they are equal partners. Do we teach children or are the children here to teach us? Learning certainly doesn't come just from books, although when I think of the thousands of books that have been read up and down this beach by all generations I am in awe—  books to lull you to sleep the way the tatatata of the sprinkler does, books to engage one in questions, books to entertain and books to laugh with, books to keep and books to throw away, books to learn from and books not to learn from. Right beside every bed and comfortable chair, there lies . . . a book. Up and down the beach on clear, fly-free days one can see people lying in hammocks whiling away the caressing summer hours with a  book. But one can read the books when one looks up and reads the storylines of the

generations: sobriety made and sobriety lost, marriages made and marriages lost, announcements of new babies conceived, and the ashes of loved ones thrown into the wind and water.

What stories the old cottages could tell! And yet, they do in our lives, lives that are never quite the same, touched forever by this place, this special place. It takes about a week for one's life to settle down, to take on the playful pulse of the place, the lapping of the lake waves on the beach, the constant chirping of the birds, and the strange noises of the night, but after about a week almost everyone calms down. Lives begin to ebb and flow rather than race. Naps with no apologies are taken, projects are started and left, short conversations and long conversations take place and no one, no one, has plans. Spontaneity becomes as familiar as the calendar of our winter years. Only tee times for golf are scheduled. In fact at the cabin it is hard to remember what day it is. Days at the cabin blend. News of the outside world is either remote or unwelcome and soon forgotten. It's strange but the cabin is a place of the now, the present. It seems strange because it is so old. Yet, it is true that the year either looks forward to the coming summer or looks back over the past summer.

For sixty years I have come to this place. It is sixty summers. It is part of my complex webbing. It is part of who I am.

My own mother came to this remote place for almost eighty years. Toward the end of her life I would help her get up here, and we would spend hours and weeks talking about the memories of this blessed haven. I do not recall one summer that I missed coming here (although there has to be one or two). After renting a cabin for many years, Grandmother received this beloved little corner of the world as a birthday present August 31, 1920, from her husband Earnest LeCompte. One of the many reasons Grandmother fell in love with this place was because she watched her frail daughter flourish in the fresh air and freedom of the cabin. The black dirt that destroys white socks offers a priceless medium for a child's imagination and spirit to soar, blossoming into robust health with the physical health soon to follow. The black dirt is embedded in the soles of my feet, feet which are tender at the first of the summer and calloused as shoe soles by the end of summer. The

black dirt is in my fingernails and the iron of the well water has run through me for a lifetime, coloring my clothes and staining my fingernails as well.

Perhaps it is the good rich dirt which makes so many of us want to garden. Perhaps we feel in some small way in partnership with the Creator. We just cannot seem to have too many flowers. For in this magical place all bloom seems possible. The color of the flowers cascading down the flower boxes and the gardens seem to express our creative joy in the place and to mask the stark reality of the bleak winters to come. In a way the cabin is like a flower needing to be cared for, showy and delicate compared to the elements that surround her. The gardens are just a small part of the coming alive of the cottages. One by one, the old places are opened like the very buds on the flowers slowly coming into full brilliance. It does not seem to matter that so much time, effort and material resources go into the very brief moment of bloom. The important thing is that both the gardens and cabins do bloom. Hope, however brief, is present and everything seems to be worthwhile. My care and love for the old place is as deep and needy as the roots of a flower and as pure and showy as its bloom. I have told the children that this is no longer just an inheritance but a legacy, a heritage. Telling them will not do the trick, though. They will have to come to that truth themselves. Nevertheless, it is a legacy that no amount of money can buy. Tell me—other than in Europe or royalty, where does one go where generations of family have worked, lived, and loved? I can close my eyes and see Mother in the back

bedroom of Kennedy's place with a big sack of popcorn and of course her mystery book. We still call the middle bedroom of the Kennedy place the yellow room although now it is white, because my mother as a child painted it yellow with a tooth brush. I have only to go to my mind's eye to see Grandmother Edna McElroy LeCompte in her long, white dress, twirling her paper parasol, walking the solitary hand mowed path through the sandy, weed grown lawns. Although I was not there, I vividly remember the stories of going down to the Pavilion of Miller's Inn for Sunday church services. The Pavilion is gone but the cement slab is still there on the lake  front property of the Theater Le Homme Dieu. Seasoned cabin owners walk in front of the cabins along the path the old road took. If one looks with imagination, you can see the ghost of the old lake front road.

Of course I have many memories of my own all connected and as real today as if they just happened. Memories race through my

mind of paper dolls, and attics on rainy days transformed in my mind into ranches and farms. I recall exploring the yet-to-be opened cottages, sneaking around corners and bushes, hiding, then being found. Always pretend, pretend, and pretend. I remember highchairs out in the yard, little picket fences to act as playpens, lemonade stands manned by budding entrepeneurs.

 As children we spent hours slapping globs of white paint on the big rocks that Grandfather as a young man had lugged up from the lake to define our driveway. Many times the painting of the rocks would end up with the painting of human bodies. Paint brushes and all finally ending up in the lake for a soaking and thorough cleaning accompanied by shrieking laugher.

Collecting "sea shells" to be dried and strung into necklaces or shells to be  painted is a fond remembrance. Memories of fishing, worm hunting, skipping rocks, games of circus, hide and seek, vague memories of turtle races and catching frogs prevail. I remember pretend

weddings, slumber parties, horseback riding, the turkey farm, and washing and drying dishes with the snapping of the wet towel. I remember sneaking a smoke on the old roof of the Dunkin garage, canoeing the path of the moon, moonlit speedboat rides, painting who loves who on the underside of the bridges connecting the chain of lakes, skinny-dipping, and old wet bathing suits dropped and pushed under the bed. I remember hours with Mother at the Laundromat with the wringer washers and the clothes line on  which we would beat the dusty Indian rugs with the broom. We used to bury the garbage and burn the trash before the garbage trucks. Memories of hikes in the woods, running from the old farm bull, pressing wild flowers, picking raspberries, working the yellow through the butter sack come into my mind like popcorn popping in the skillet.

There are lots of memories of bedtime. Darkness will transform this playground. There are memories of stories both listened to and told from tales of scary Kings who cut off the heads of their wives to stories of homing pigeons with instincts  to take them safely home. Snuggled in the safe but always funny smelling beds of the

cabin we would draw lakes on each others backs. Remembering boyfriends at late night beaches, floating in boats in the middle of a moonlit night (trying I am sure to attract the boys) and roller skating at the Gang Plank, I smile. I remember trying not to wake anyone sneaking the car out, rolling it quietly down the drive until it would hit the white rocks that lined the way and glowed in the moonlight. The noise we made should have woken everyone up and down the beach and probably did. I remember sleeping in tents, sleeping under full moons, sleeping so soundly in the fresh open air. Sleeping . . . only to arise at noon when we as teenagers would pull on our swimsuits and start all over again. As children we didn't need many clothes because we would go from swimsuits to pajamas playing on and in the water all day.

From my childhood to my own children always to the lake we would go. What a lake it is! Oh, how wonderful is the look of surprise that dissolves the flicker of anxiousness on the trusting faces of children as they first learn to ski with supportive adults all cheering on the shore. The startled squeal of the three-year-old when a fish first bites his line is an experience each seasoned lake person knows well. We are drawn by the magic

and the mystique of the lake. We love this lake where there are no snakes, just rocks to skip, sand to clean and build with and weeds where great fish swim. This magical lake, where my sixteen-year-old mother swam and almost drowned in a surprise storm, has a mind of its own. My mother and a boyfriend named Ed took off to swim the lake on an absolutely beautiful and calm day with Aunt Edith paddling alongside in the red canoe. They had almost accomplished their mission to reach the other side of the lake when a fierce and sudden thunderstorm came over the region forcing the frightened and exhausted swimmers to turn back and swim with the waves, not against them. Of course, the canoe was swept away. The young people were not hurt but were very scared. They spent hours and hours

 fighting the waves before they were washed up on shore. Totally exhausted beyond imagination the swimmers were to spend the next few days in bed before they recovered the strength to walk. This is the stormy lake which dislodges docks and pounds our toys both big and small into its foam. In the early days before telephones of any kind or public shore patrols, each cabin fireplace mantle would have an important hand-held bell to ring. If there was danger on the lake, the occupants of the cabins would stand by the water's edge ringing the bells to send the alarming alert to all

the men along the way who had boats that there was danger on the lake and someone was in trouble. Then there is the calm lake, the lake like glass. The ultimate prize was finding just the "perfect" rock to skip not once, but four and five times over the glassy water. Then there is the fun lake that rolls our inner  tubes over and over, again and again, into giant white caps. The fun lake that catches us as we release from rope swings and blows our sailboats from shore to shore. The clean spring and rainwater filled lake that the glacier sculpted so long ago. Water, life giving water that has minnows nipping at our feet, water that can be so wonderful at times, and so frightening at other times, washes over us claiming us as its own. The water that reflects rainbows, pink clouds and orange moons, and more often than not, reflects double rainbows, fuchsia clouds and Northern lights, etches its essence into our beings.

Naturally something has to remind us that this is only paradise as we know it, not as God knows it. That job is left to what we call the state bird—the mosquito. The wretched, pesky mosquito who is always ready to disrupt stargazing, picnics, late night bonfires, and if possible, a good night's sleep. No wonder I have such elation when I reduce that

buzzing pest to a bloody splat on my arm. Just as mosquitoes are around, not all memories are sweet. Perhaps that is to jar us out of complacency. Whatever the reason, "shit" is the great fertilizer of faith. I think it was Erma Bombeck who noticed the grass was greener over the septic tank. There is a strange thing about sad memories though . . . they fade as the years pass. The years file away the rough edges of the pain. Like the memories of the summer of 1954 when I got the dreaded disease called polio, which was crippling children all over the country. Upon diagnosis of polio, I was whisked away from my beloved lake and placed in an old hospital house in a corner room in complete isolation for one month. Now we all know and realize that there were tears, fears, and scares, the whole gamut of hell for an eleven-year-old not to mention a frantic parent, but for the life of me, all I can remember is my little toy clown and all the cards and letters I got. I do remember my mother's face in the window of the door. I remember in my mind's eye chasing the bad polio army with my good army up and down my body willing the bad army not to make camp. It is strange, but, all in all, the memories are good. Perhaps that is because I had no paralysis. I did learn a valuable life lesson, and that was to embrace solitude and to be at one with loneliness. All the cousins and children on the beach had to have huge shots which they repeatedly reminded me of when I was released from

the hospital. That was the same summer the bungalow burnt down from a direct hit of lightning from one of our infamous electrical storms. The lightening hit the wires and fire ran to the bungalow. My, what an exciting summer that was. It sure must have held a lot of tears and hard work but all I can remember is how popular I was and the new bungalow we got. Dad spent most of the insurance money from the fire remodeling the main cabin. Dad was around a lot more that summer and filled the cabin with fifties wrought iron and modern stuff, all of which has long since gone. During the summer most of the Southern men on the beach would fly or drive back and forth from their homes, allowing the women and children to stay out of the brutal summer heat of Kansas, Nebraska, Oklahoma and Texas. This is what the men who had preceded them had done, but now with computers both the men and women are able to keep up with their jobs here at the cabin. Air conditioning was just coming into its own in the fifties.

Then there is the memory of food, food cooked over a wood stove, in an oven, or

on a gas grill. Mother tells the stories of the dairy truck from an old nearby farm that would lumber down the road twice a week with

fresh milk and eggs. Once a week another neighbor's farm cart rolled down the back road, delivering to the lake people a variety of fresh vegetables taken right out of the ground. On Sundays, as a special treat, many lakeshore families would venture up to Miller's Inn, which is now the Theater Le Homme Dieu, to indulge in brunch or go down Tolena Road for Smorgasbord at the Tolena Club. Food eaten at Andy's Interlaken Inn while playing the Bear is such a fun memory. Onion rings and hash browns, which the South cannot do but the North does to perfection is a memory. Dinners at Chets, dinners at the Corral, dinners at the Depot, the Downtowner, Herbies—all or most of them specialize in walleye and chicken. We have partaken of most of all the discount "specials," such as the Buck Burgers at Herbies, two dollar breakfasts at the Depot and dollar burgers at The Mercantile, mainly to take in the local color of the region. Throughout the week many neighbors can be seen dining at Jim's Interlachen Inn. In the past it was considered a treat to eat out. Now it is a treat to eat a home-cooked meal, but either way, the eating places are all part of our heritage. Of course we all remember the food at the Fourth of July celebrations where the shore people can picnic by the lake and feast on medium or medium rare hamburgers that the government now forbids restaurants to serve. The fireworks were a sight to see! The flares bursting in air reflected on the water make one's heart swell with pride and gratitude.

For years it seemed like every summer we or someone along the shores would make what we called our annual trip to the emergency ward resenting every moment of our time away from the lake. There would be rope burns from skiing, cut fingers from cooking projects, rusty nails from building or tearing down, something lodged in the eye or an eye infection or some infection sending us scurrying to the hospital. Along with the bad memories one would throw in the bats in the rafters (Grandmother used to hang parasols upside down to keep the little guys up there), mouse tracks in linen drawers and broken everything—steps, chairs, boats, mowers, swings and hammocks all needing mending and replacing. Like the aging body I guess that is part of "old." Sometimes the fixed is better than the original but what a hassle. Yet, what a privilege! I do laugh with wonder why with age we want our personal body to look like new but the 'old' fixed up cabin to look like the charming old. Must be one of those confusions the world wants us to believe.

The young generation is very quick to throw out the old, like the round early American coffee table at Kennedy's cabin which was my mother's first wedding present. I guess you don't throw out the memory when you throw the piece away but you sure throw out the reminder of that memory and eventually the memory is lost. It really is my mother's memory not

mine, or is it? I think my memory is the listening to my elderly mother telling me stories and looking into those old faded, baby blue eyes and seeing the sparkle of the new bride as she tells me all about her first wedding gift. My old mother . . . the cabin takes on the qualities of an older mother. The cabin has an intense nurturing about her which feeds us, exercises us, calms us and reassures us. That motherly  strength, that rallies in times of crisis and prods gently at laziness almost to the point of her depletion, is unyielding. The old cabin certainly defines loyalty. She is always here to ground us and to point out how to read and redirect our lives just like a mother teaching her young child to read. "See here," she says. "See that, see this. Learn, play and enjoy!" says the old cabin. "Never, never make the mistake of thinking that this, that I, can be bought with money," she informs us. Loyalty can  not be bought. It is a gift just as love is or it is not loyalty at all, but a bribe. The world will want to bribe us with the "take the money and run" thinking, but the old cottage can offer those of us who are blessed enough to receive the gift of

love and loyalty, life with value. Like the umbilical cord she attaches us to what is important in life—to life itself. Pumping us with the characteristics of integrity, loyalty, honesty and love, the old cabin ties us to those eternal qualities running through past generations. Then too, like bad memories, the character defects are lost and only the good goes on. This tying us to the past happens every day. I will go to hang a flowering pot of petunias and there in just the right spot is an old rusty forgotten nail showing me where someone long ago hung a similar plant. Each and every time I lug the hose and sprinklers out I reflect on the generations of men, women and children that hauled the backbreaking watering buckets up from the lake to water those now towering trees I so enjoy. A shimmering, rhythmic, red canoe goes by and I remember my mother's high school graduation present, which I so carelessly left out one winter only to find it gone in the summer. Every year in the sand on the beach, I catch a glimpse of an old crumbled retaining wall or boat house that the relentless winter ice has destroyed. These are projects  embarked upon by ancestors intent on holding the damaging substance back . . . but of course, they cannot. The lake takes and the lake returns. Sandy beaches are created one year, only to turn into foot crippling rocks the following year.

Although, I can testify that the lake has never returned all those little outboard motors that have been accidentally dropped into the lake over the past decades, much less the other paraphernalia. I am anchored to the past when I watch children roll and dust and paint the big white rocks that Grandfather and the other cabin men hauled and collected from the lake. At one time for years the white rocks lined the shores of those industrious folks as if to tell all who passed by that "THIS IS FAMILY." These families of folks from all over the country are linked together by tears and laughter. They are linked together by the cabins themselves. Walking through comparable life experiences honoring each other's journey, we are bonded. As blood bonds the family, so this sharing bonds the neighbors. We are so blessed to experience this family of neighbors who calm our anxieties and see the beauty and possibilities in each other. They give so much. Neighbors acting like family, challenging sorrow and loving goodness, make the time spent at the lake so very beautiful and such a joyous place to be.

Sometimes I think that being at the cabin is just a time to give and work. So much hard work has to be done and there are many things which have to be maintained and kept up, but the cabin also offers an opportunity to receive. I used to think that I didn't deserve this old, beloved cabin, and I certainly could not

figure out how God was going to select the right family members to own it—family members that would love it as I thought it should be loved. Through inheritance, and being ready to buy and respond, I received. I now realize that in the receiving of the gift, I become deserving of breathing in her sweet beauty, touching her softness as well as her rough spots, smelling all of her un- familiar smells from mildew to lilacs. I can see her charm through the veil of chipped paint, slanted floors and leaky roofs. Through all of my senses, I am worthy to love her because I chose to receive her.

Oh my . . . How the old place can make itself heard. Because the cabins are not insulated and not sealed tightly hardly a sound does not make it into the cabin. As parents we use to eavesdrop on our unsuspecting children, hearing everything as they chattered away in a boat out on the lake on a calm evening. The squeaking of the boat cranks, the purring of a distant motor boat, the bark of a dog, the nearby screeching of an owl, the rush and scurry of squirrels over the wood deck, are all sounds that make their way to my senses. The far off sound of a lonely train whistle calls me to remember memories not long ago lived of another time and another place and another person. The slapping of

a speedboat against the water, the lapping of the waves, and the rustle of the cottonwood trees as they toss in the breeze are not lost. Oh, I can hear the chirp of the birds, always the birds: the squawk of the blackbirds at noon and the low, unforgettable, wailing call of the loons in the evening. The loons are calling to somewhere deep in our souls. Do you hear the whirl of the ceiling fans, the calling of the distant train, and the sound of a far off car rushing somewhere passing everywhere? I can hear the slam of the car door as "they" return from golfing or shopping, a far off greeting from a neighbor painting a mailbox, or the serious chatter and raucous laughter of walkers on the back road. Oh, yes, I can hear the grind of the lawnmowers and the weedeaters as they sprinkle the lawns with fresh cut grass. What is that irritating clinking noise? It is the sound of the cleat on the rope of the flagpole that carries our country's flag as well as our state 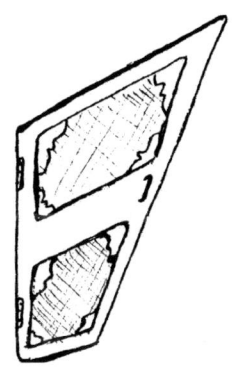 flags and often football championship flags, flag poles that pranksters often fly underwear from. I can hear the patter of little feet on the wood floors and the click of the dog's paws as he stands at the door to be let in.

"Let in" is a partnership of calling and opening that old screen door. "Let in." We all want to be let in to the old cabin. As if to be let in we are brought back home, wrapped in a sun-drenched towel warming our cold bodies, let in as if we belong, as if we are never on the outside looking in but are always welcome and belonging to the inside. Do we get smug thinking we are the inside group? Do we own the key, the key to the inside? Maybe, but then we realize that it is not us who make up the inside group, but the soul of the old mother cabin. She and only she dictates who is deserving and who isn't, and we know that it is in the receiving of the gift of the old cabin that we become deserving. She gives and we receive.

With this blessing of receiving comes the other side of the coin, and that is responsibility. Responsibilities to hear her call, respond to her call, preserve her call and history, and then finally to have our lives transformed, imprinted by her very being. The cabins are filled with this being, filled with picture albums, pictures on walls of honored past guests, inventories of her possessions, memorabilia of all kinds, like the stuffed fish caught years ago when fishing was an art and men wore ties and jackets to fish in, needlepoint pillows keeping shut-in fingers busy, quilts which are still so beloved they aren't used. It is funny how quilts began by taking unused old pieces and out of necessity making them a thing

of warmth. Now they are no longer necessary but of more value than all the blankets we could buy over a lifetime. We place old-fashioned oil lamps around the cottage reminding us of a time when light was dictated to us mostly by nature, not

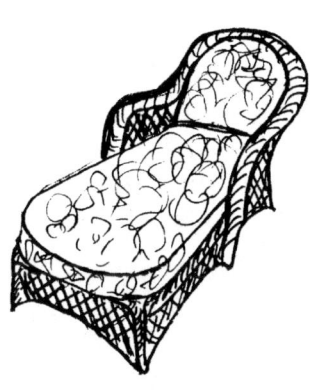 power lines. There are crocheted pieces draped over the arms of chairs and couches to catch the dirt before the time of spot removers and dry cleaning. Now if they get dirty (the crocheted pieces) we carefully hand wash them. They even look a little tacky now, but, nevertheless, there it is the crocheted piece over the head of Grandmother's old wicker chaise lounge where both she and I have spent so many hours together, linked in time by only the chaise and the crocheted piece. I was two years old when Grandmother died. I never knew her and yet, I do know her. I wonder if my grandchildren will have such thoughts as they casually place their heads on the needlepoint pillows some lady long ago spent summers doing. It doesn't matter. It was in the process of making the pillows that thrilled me, not the end product. How often we forget that we are human beings not human doings. The cabin too just is. She doesn't really do anything but we care about her. Sometimes what we care about most, what

we treasure most gets all used up and goes away . . . never to return. So, while we have her, it's best we love her, care for her, fix her up when she breaks, and heal her when she is sick. Then and only then do we reap the benefit of how she blesses us.

Like memories . . .

woolgathering continues . . .

indulged in by Beth Dunkin